Adult Coloring Book For Gen X 80's Slang

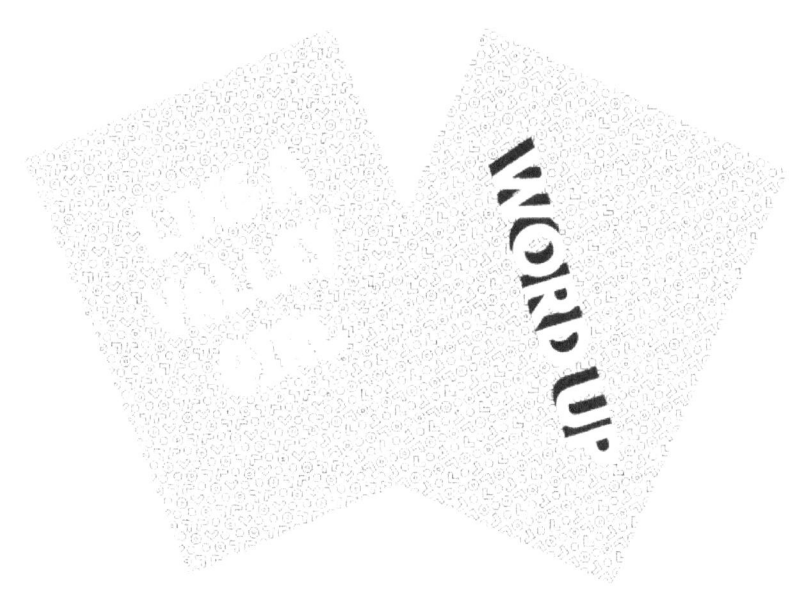

COPYRIGHT 2021

Missy Publishing
Kat Robarge

COPYRIGHT 2021

Missy Publishing
Kat Robarge

The adult coloring book trend has spread nationwide. Why is this? The reason is people can get many health benefits from coloring for example:
- REDUCE STRESS AND ANXIETY
- IMPROVE MOTOR SKILLS AND VISION
- IMPROVE SLEEP
- IMPROVE FOCUS

With all of this said maybe it is time to grab a glass of wine (or Zima) a few colored pencils (neon if you can find them) your glasses (If you grew up in the '80s like I did, you need them), and this funny flashback to the '80s coloring book to reduce your stress, no need to be an artist just color the pages any way you like. Enjoy volume one. I plan on creating a few more.

COPYRIGHT 2021

Missy Publishing
Kat Robarge

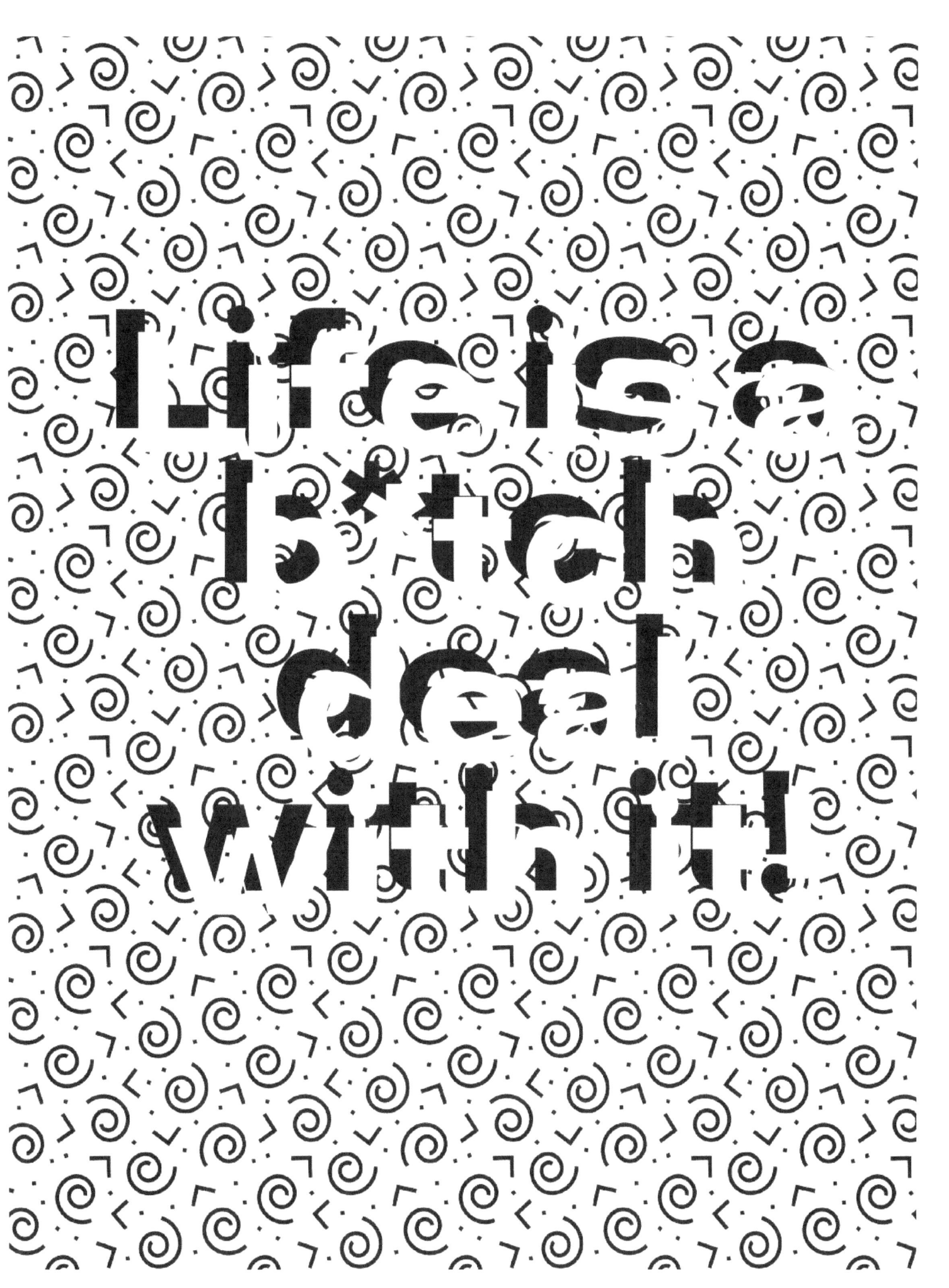

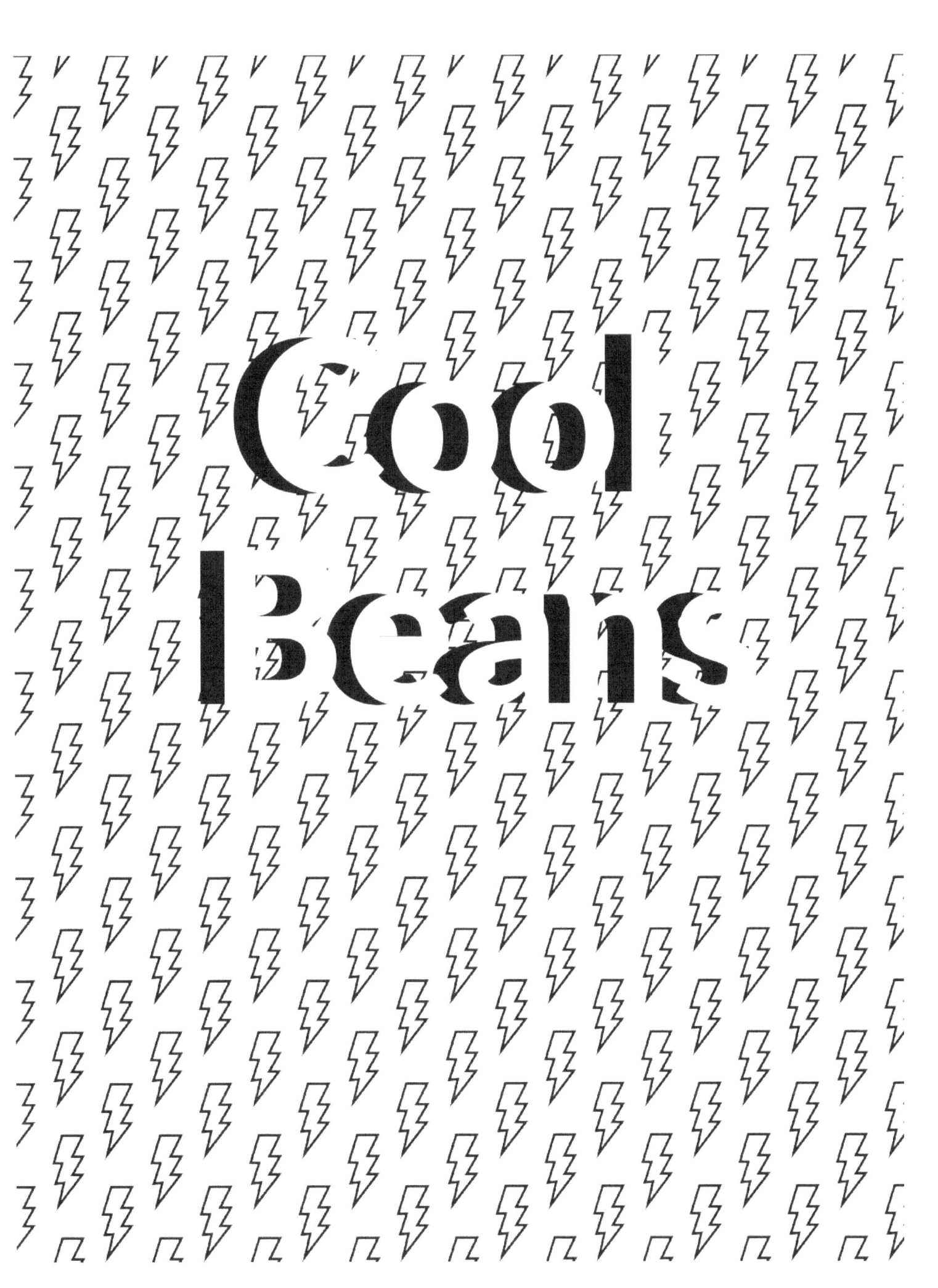

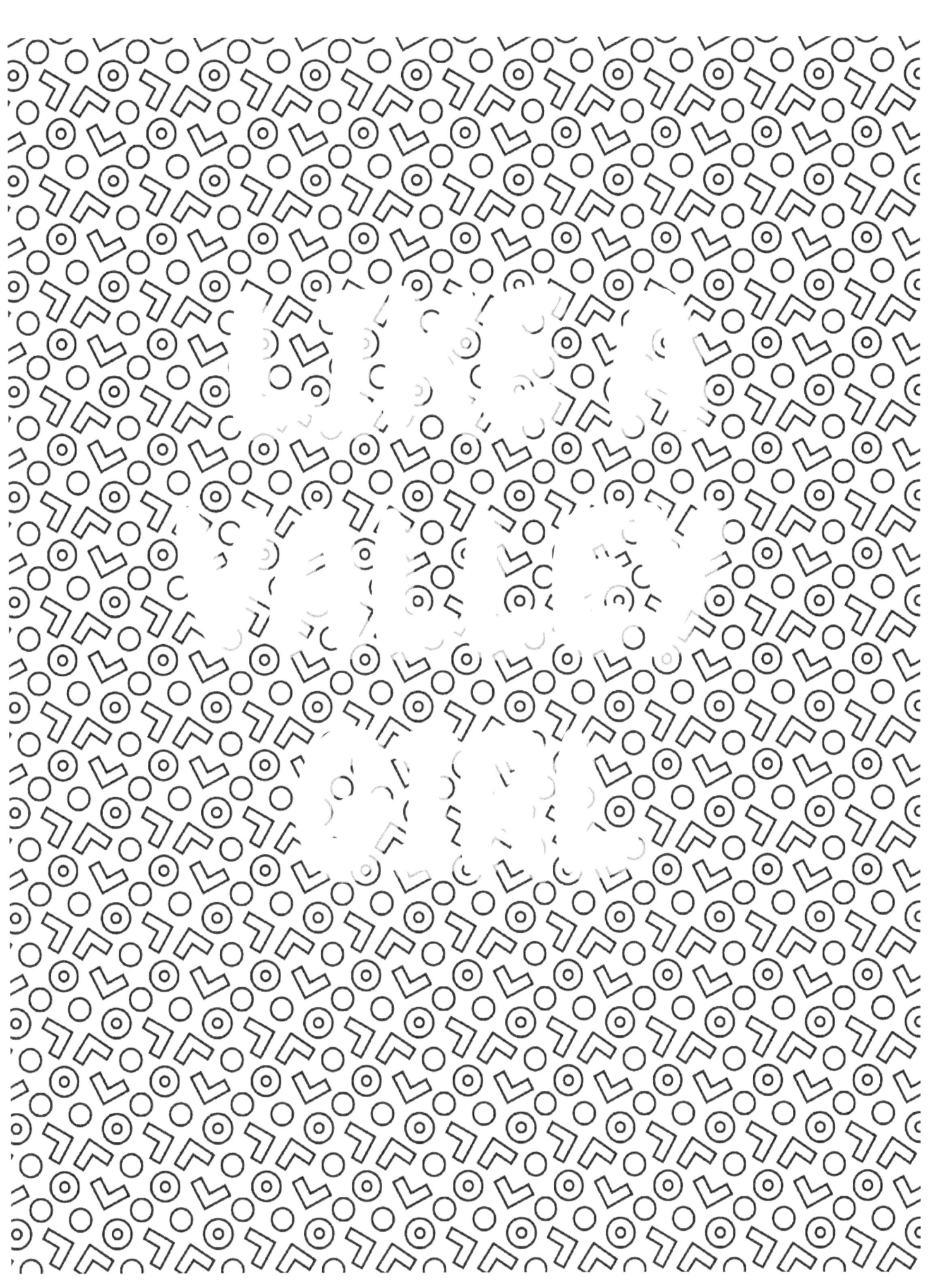

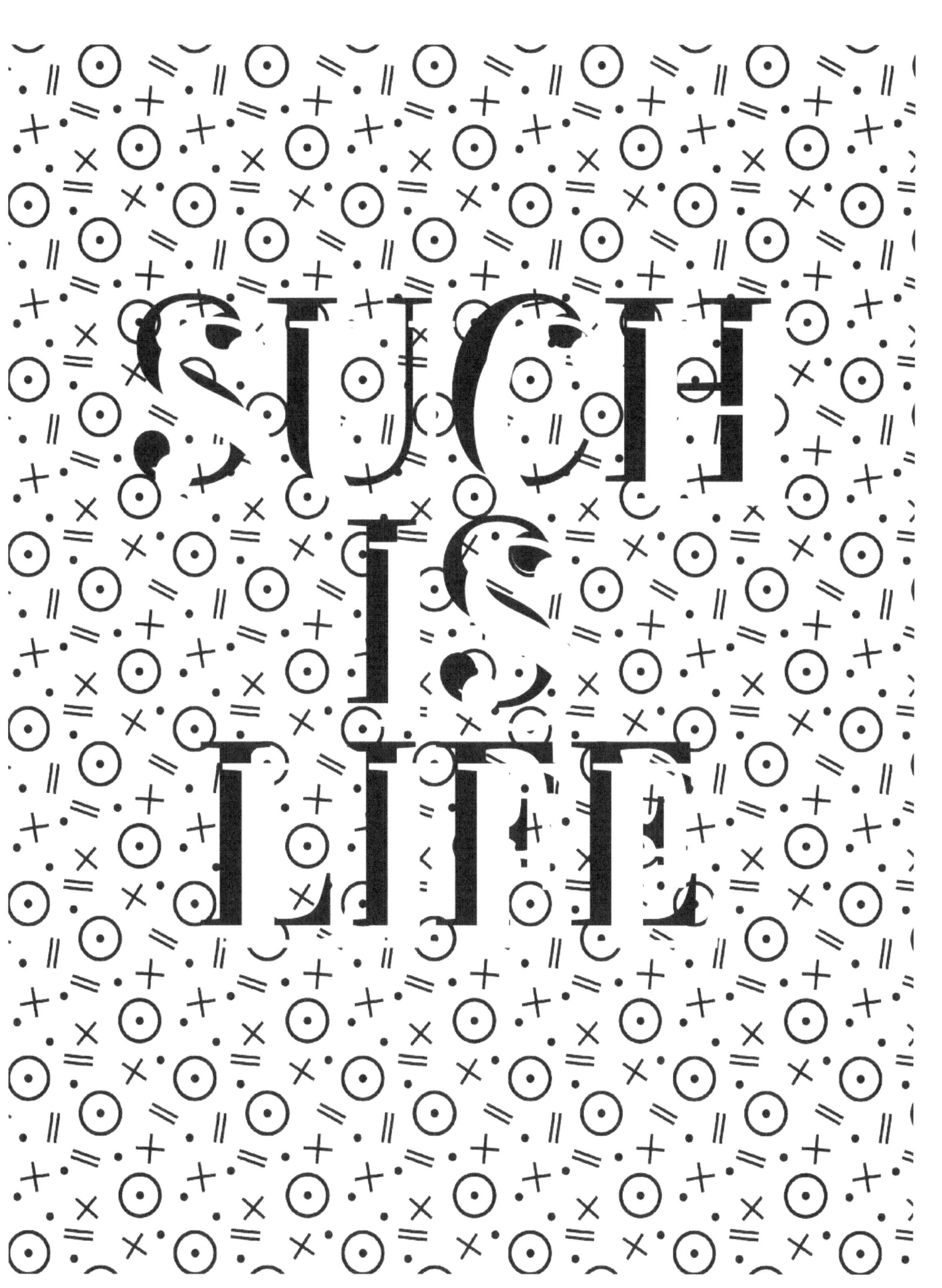

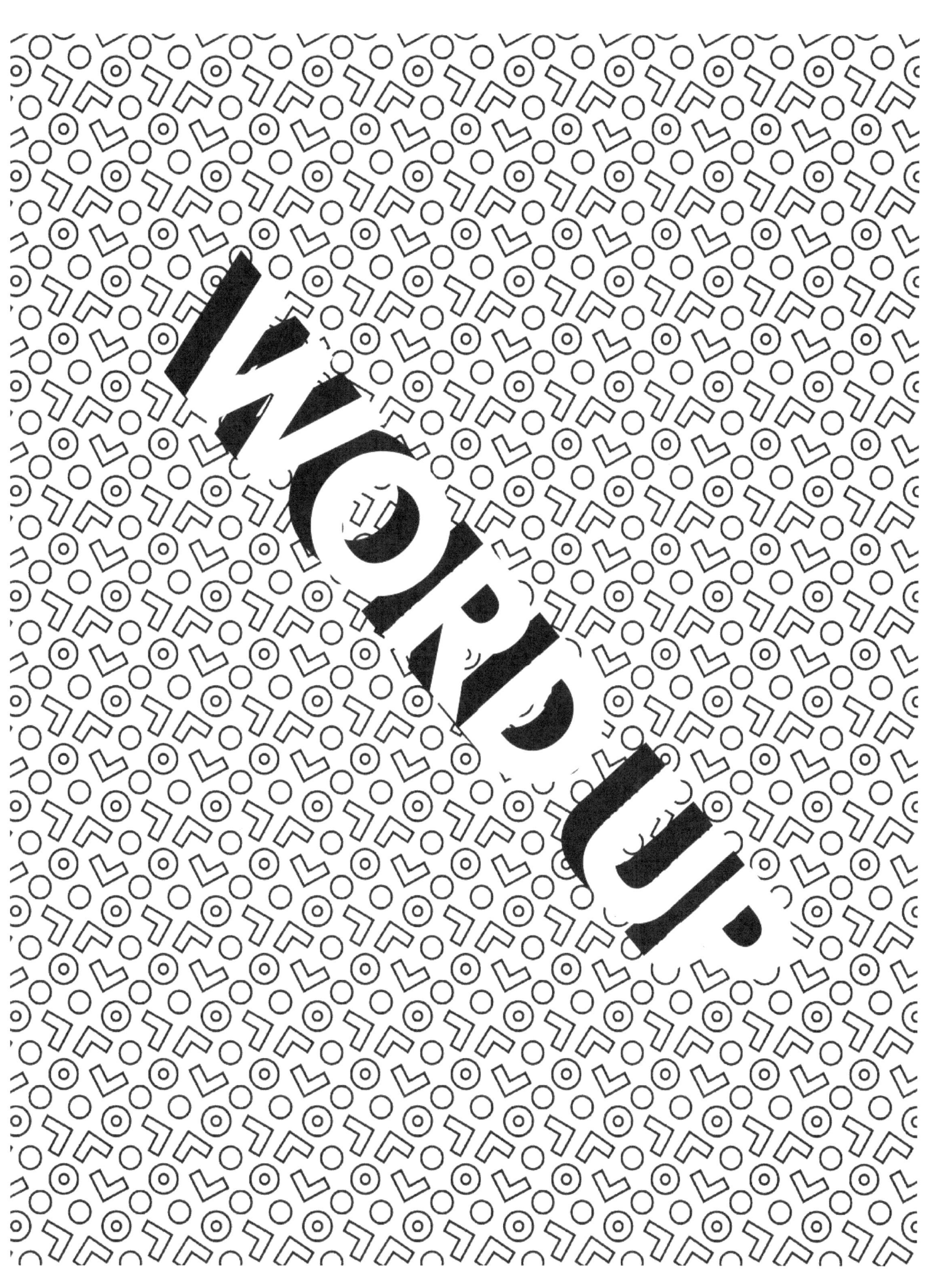

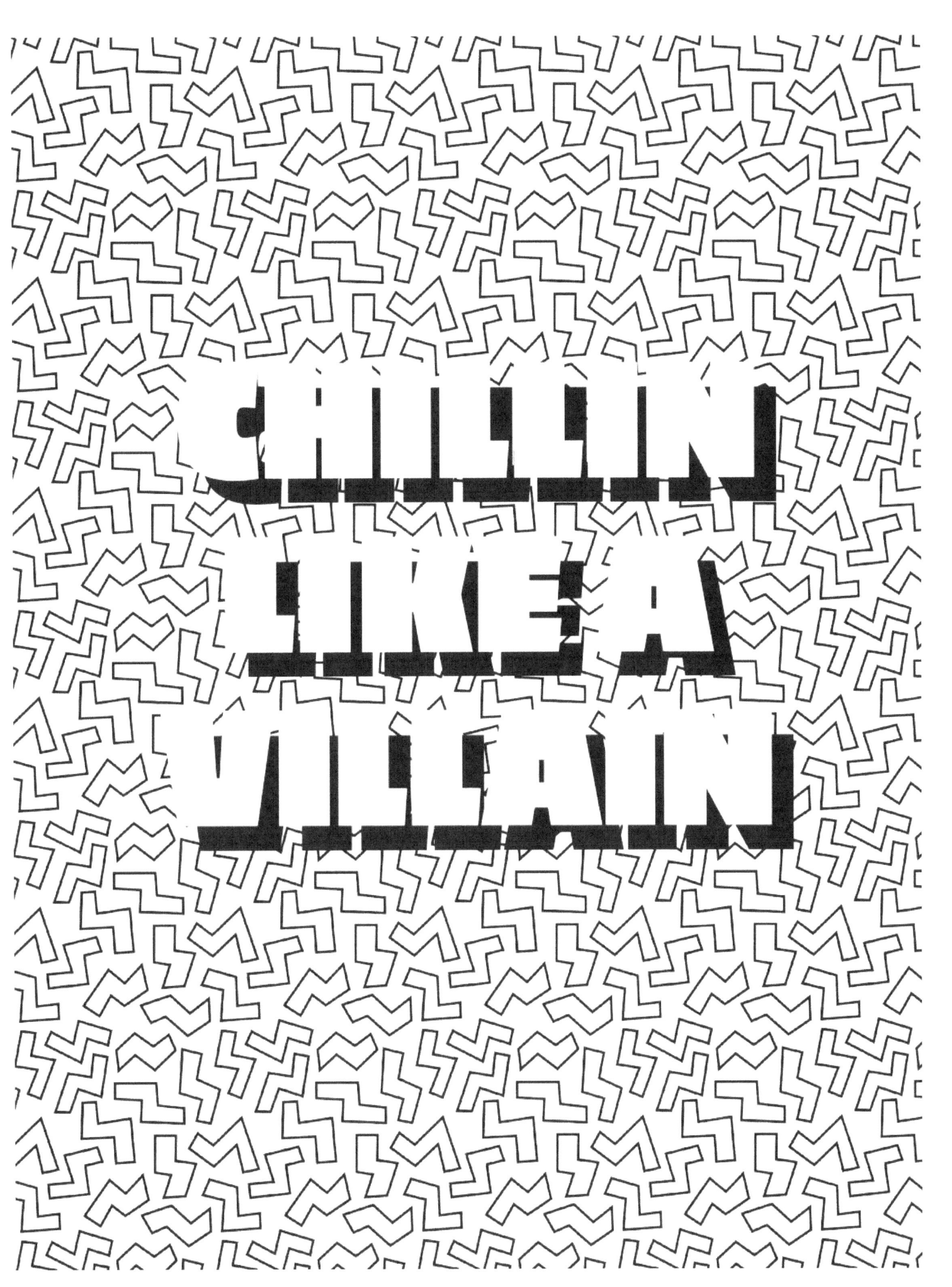

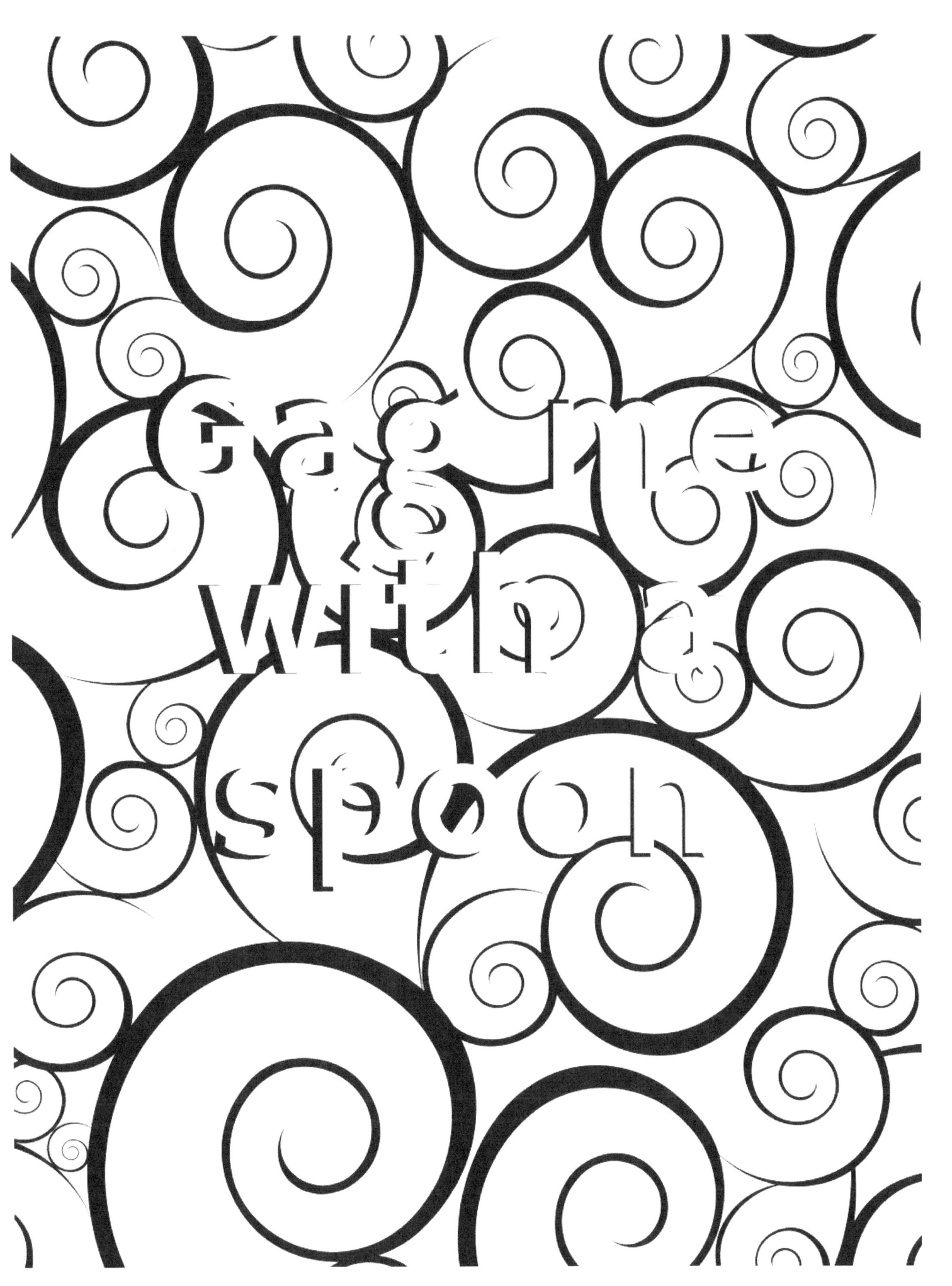

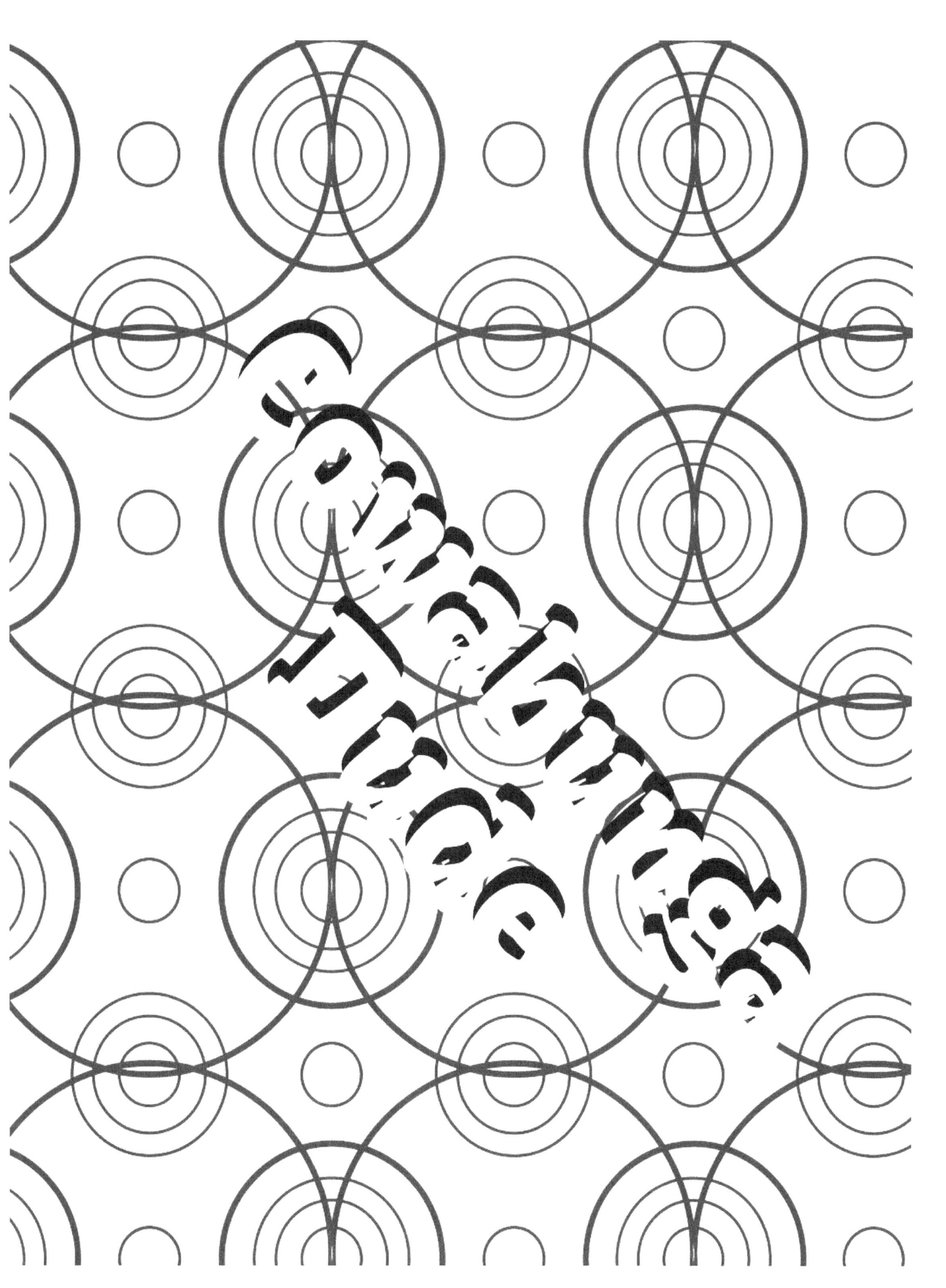

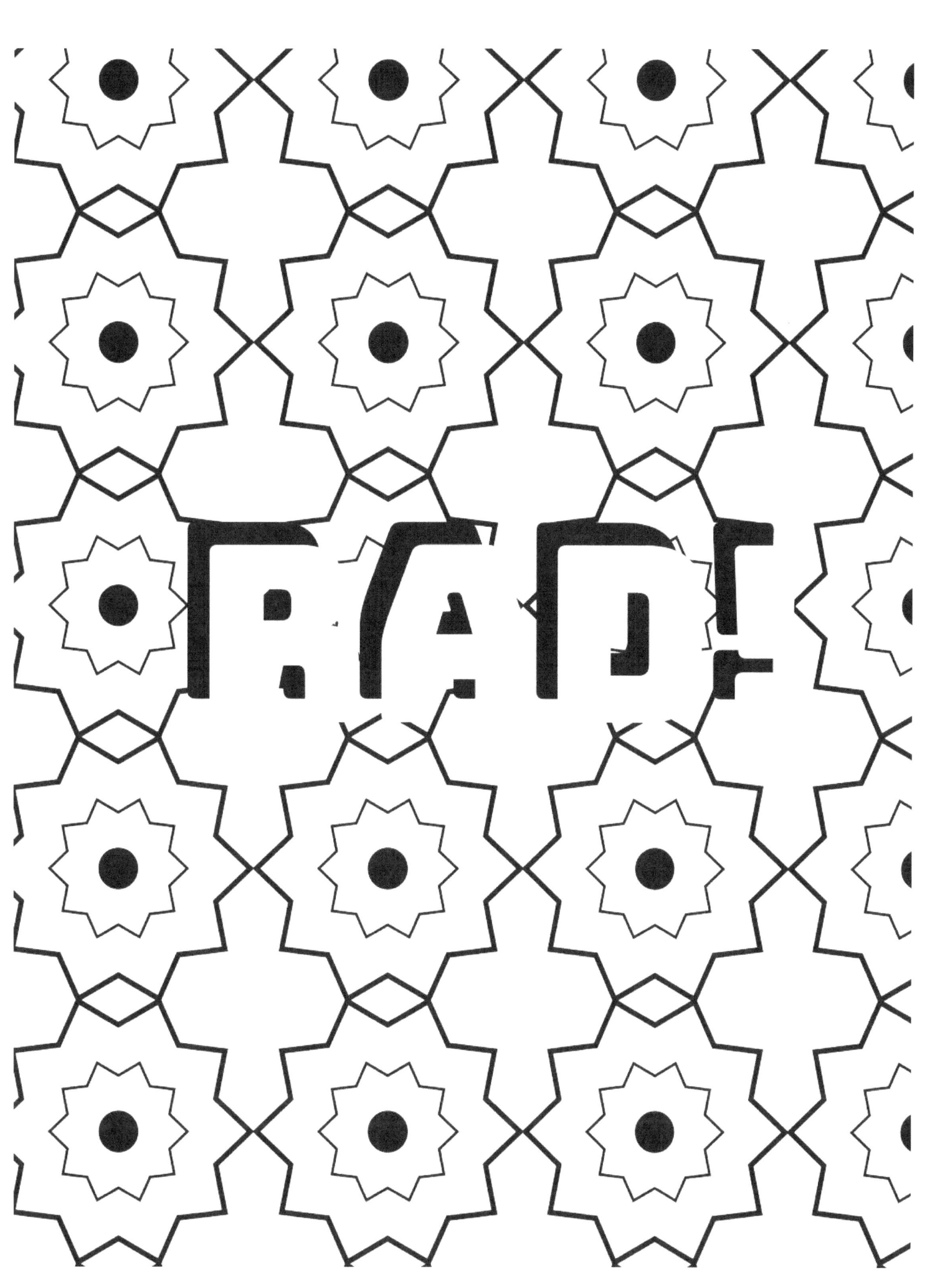

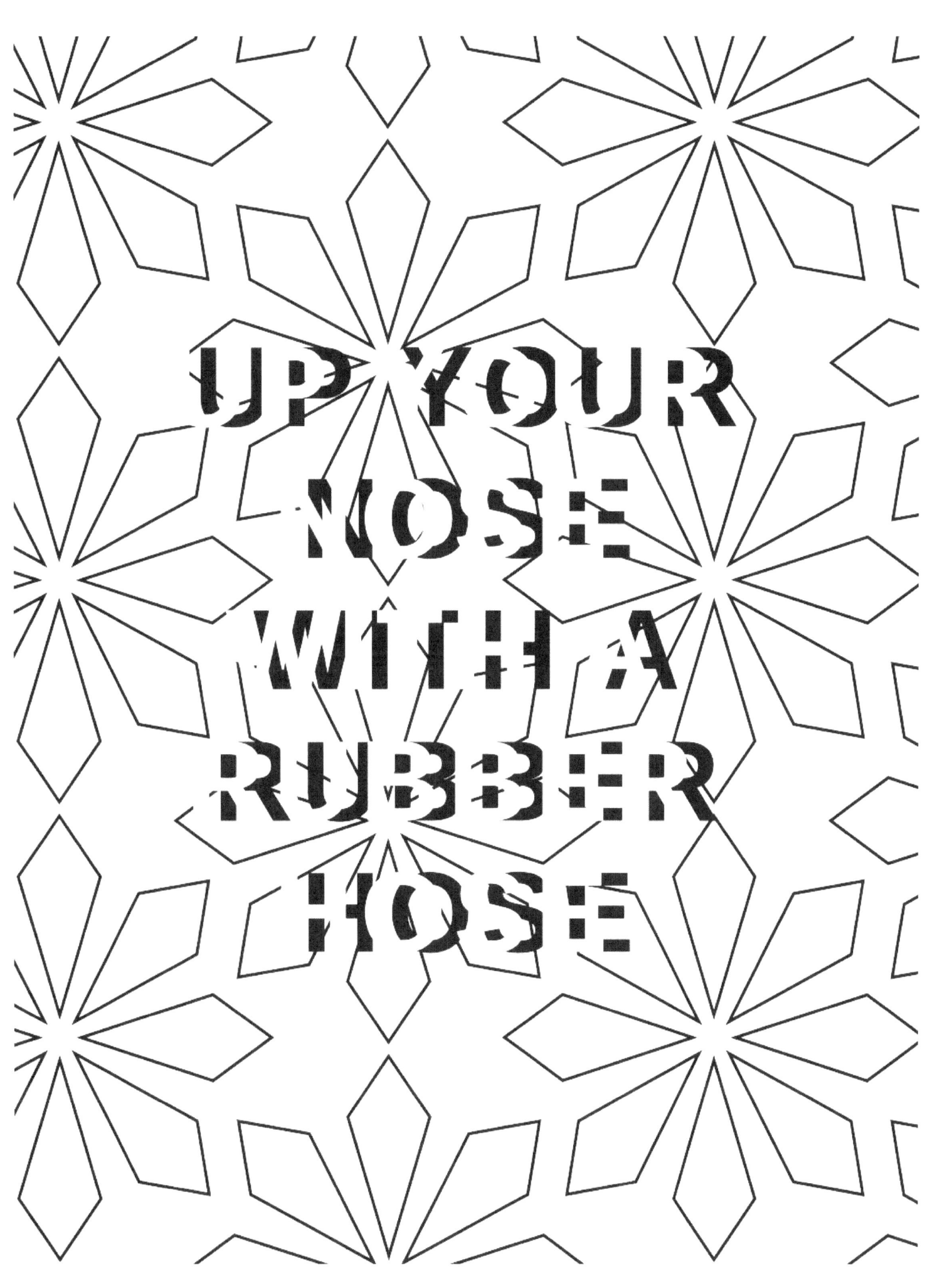

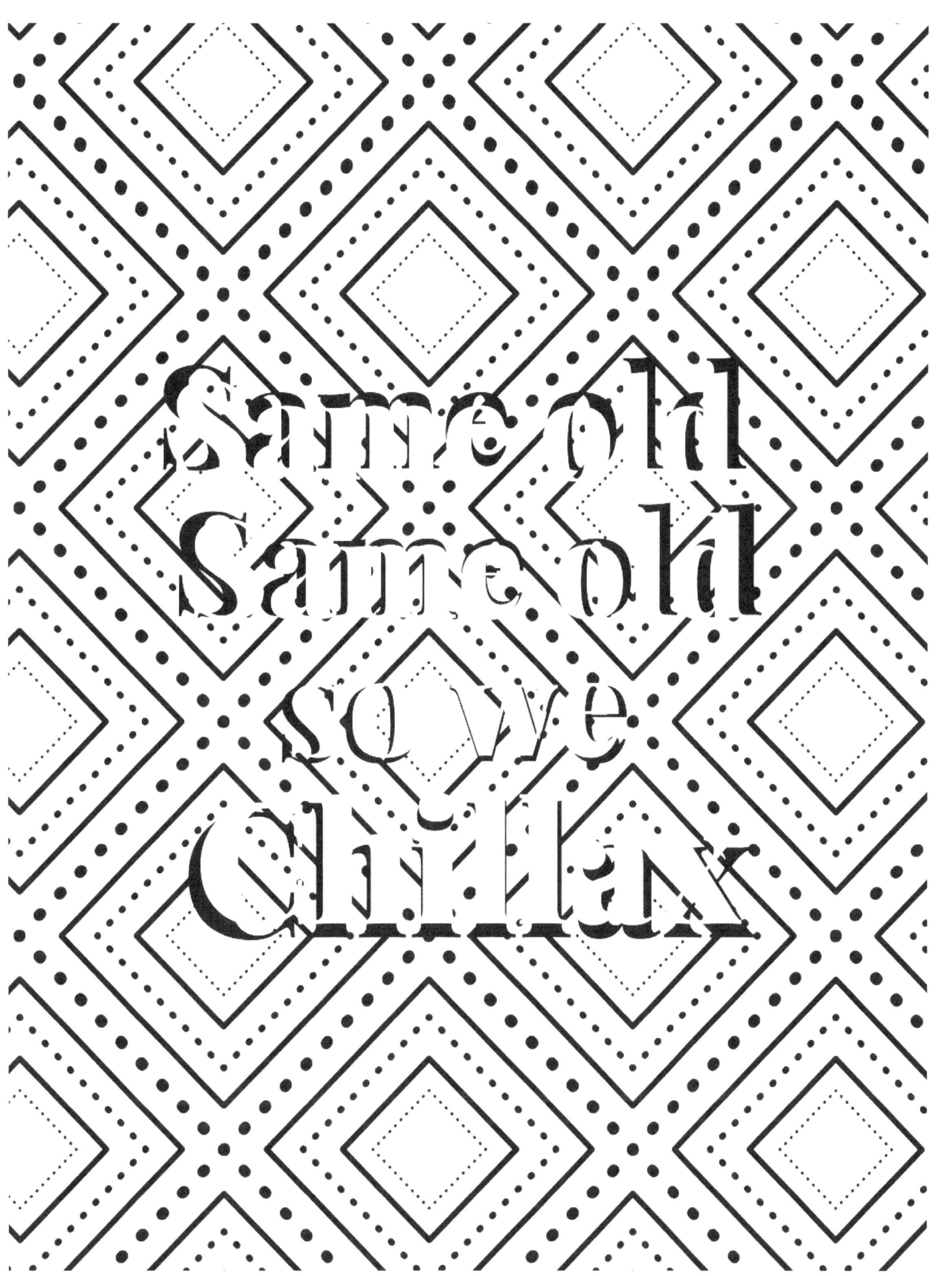

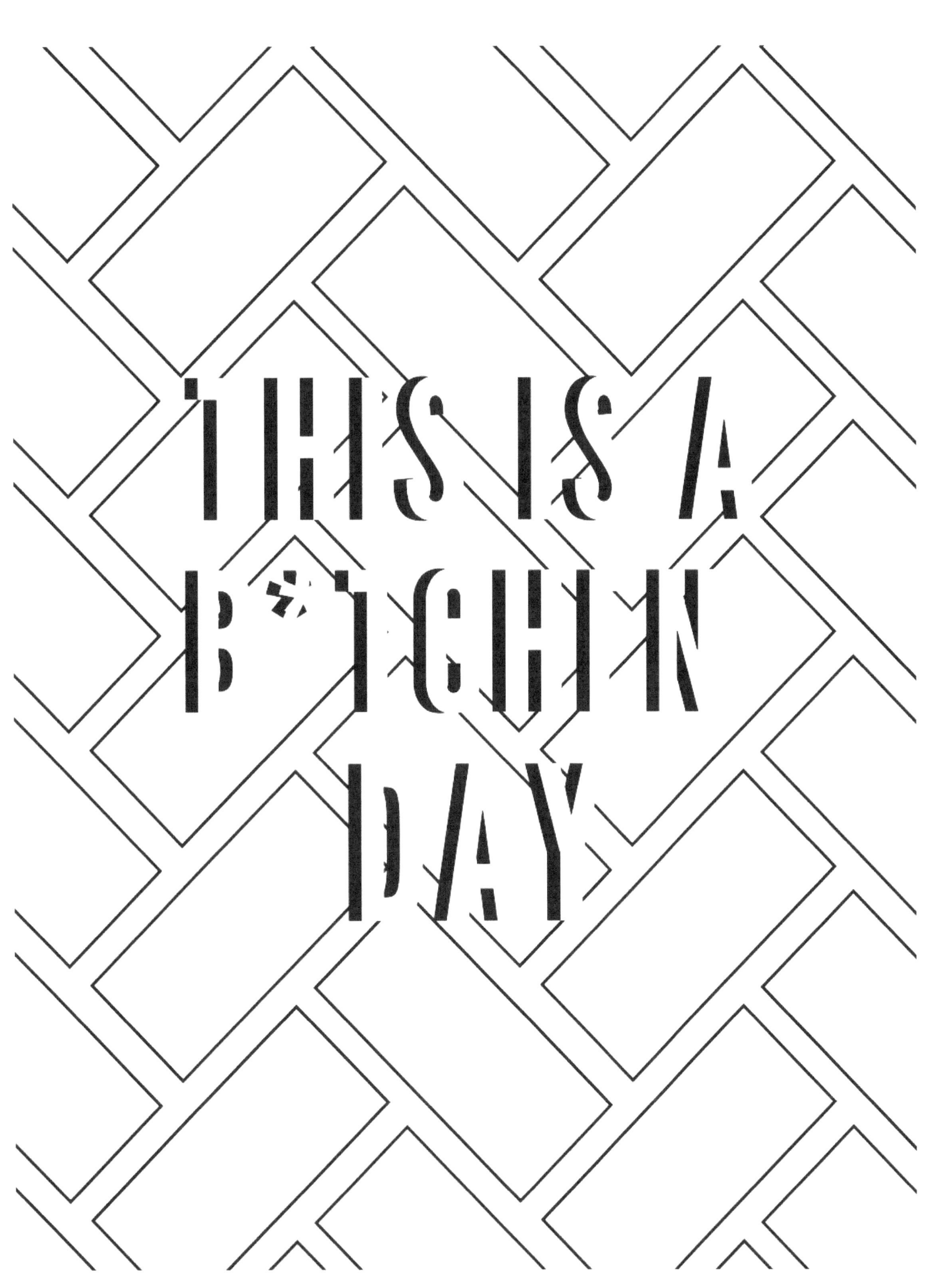

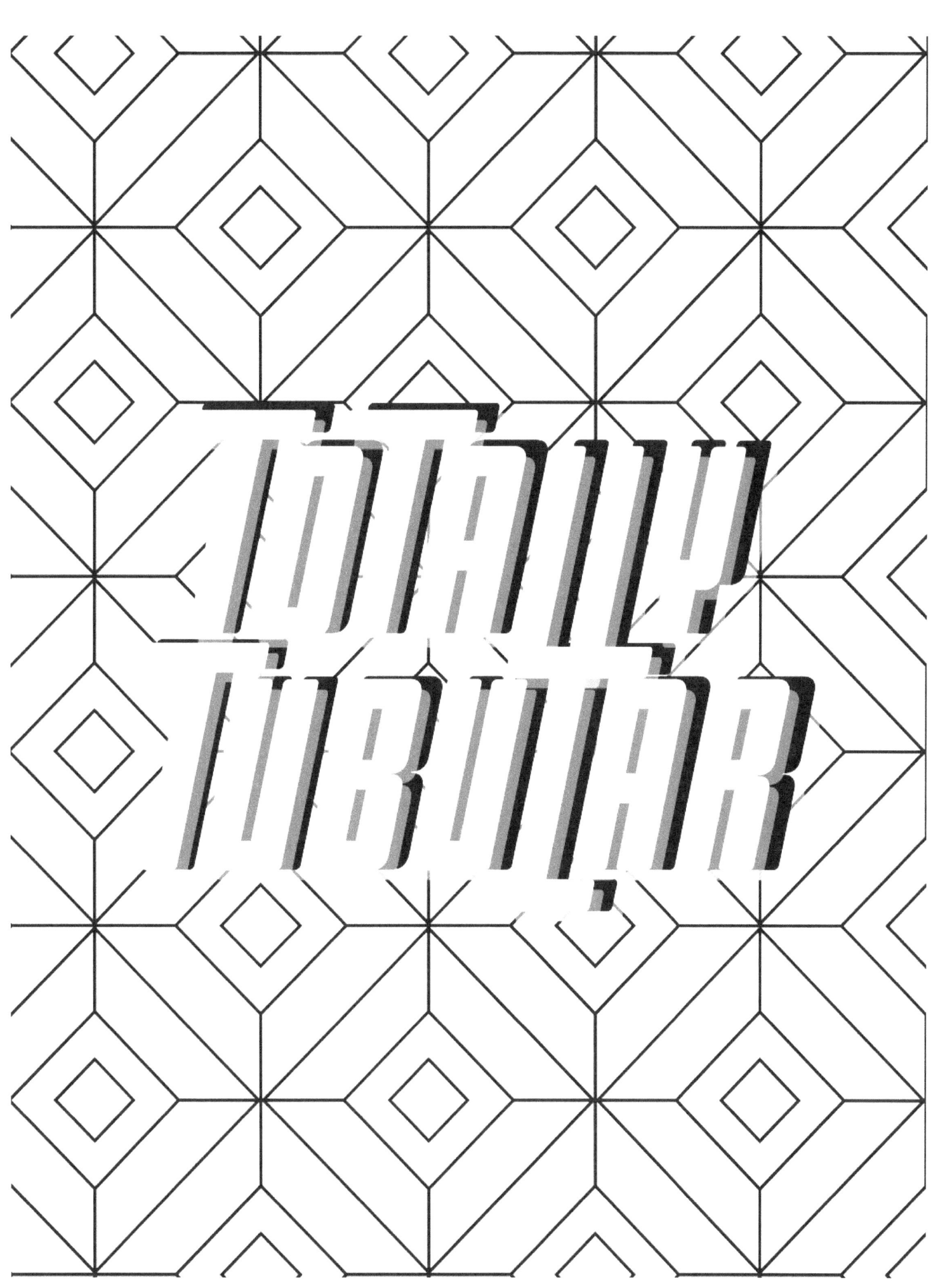

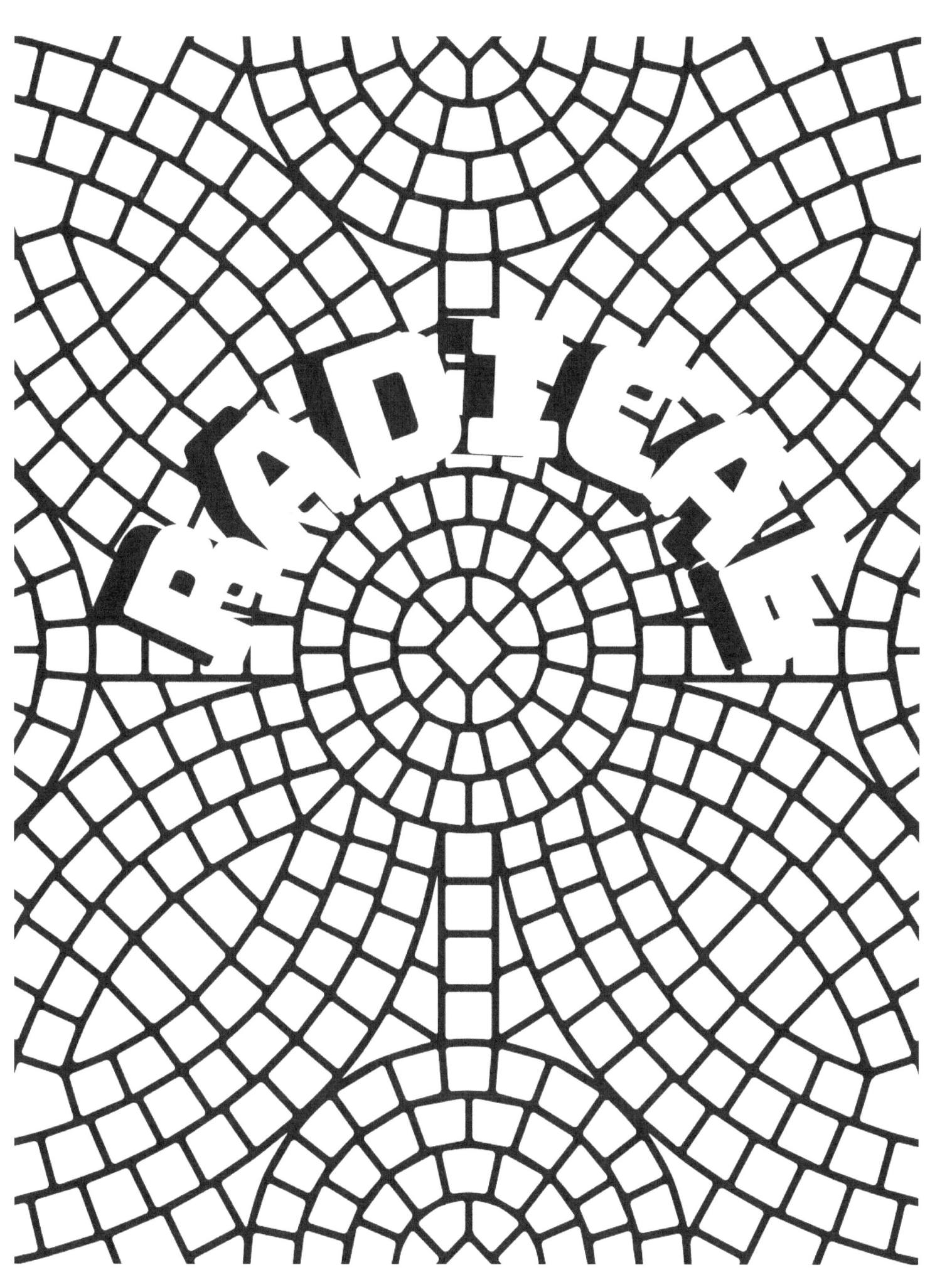

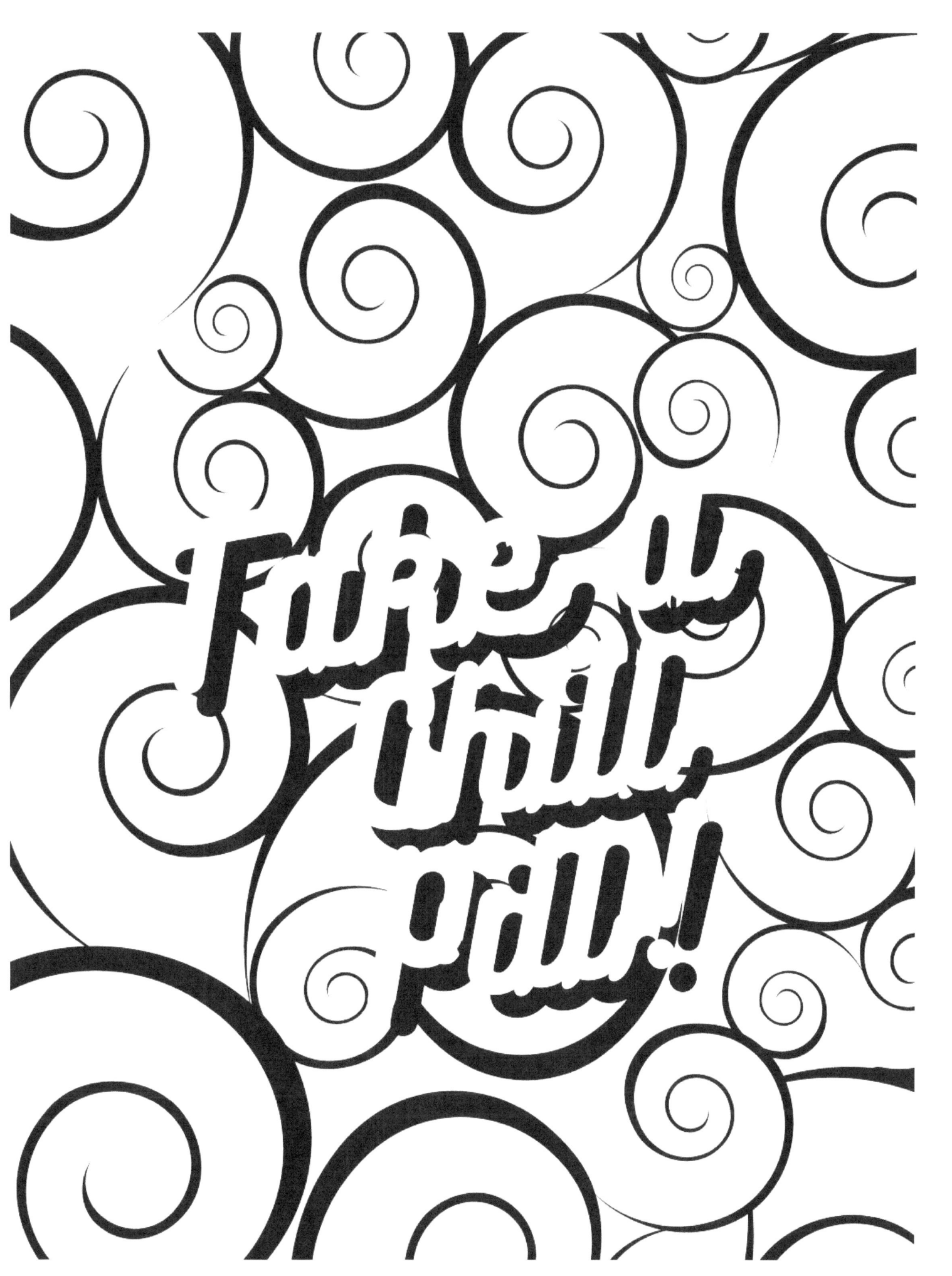

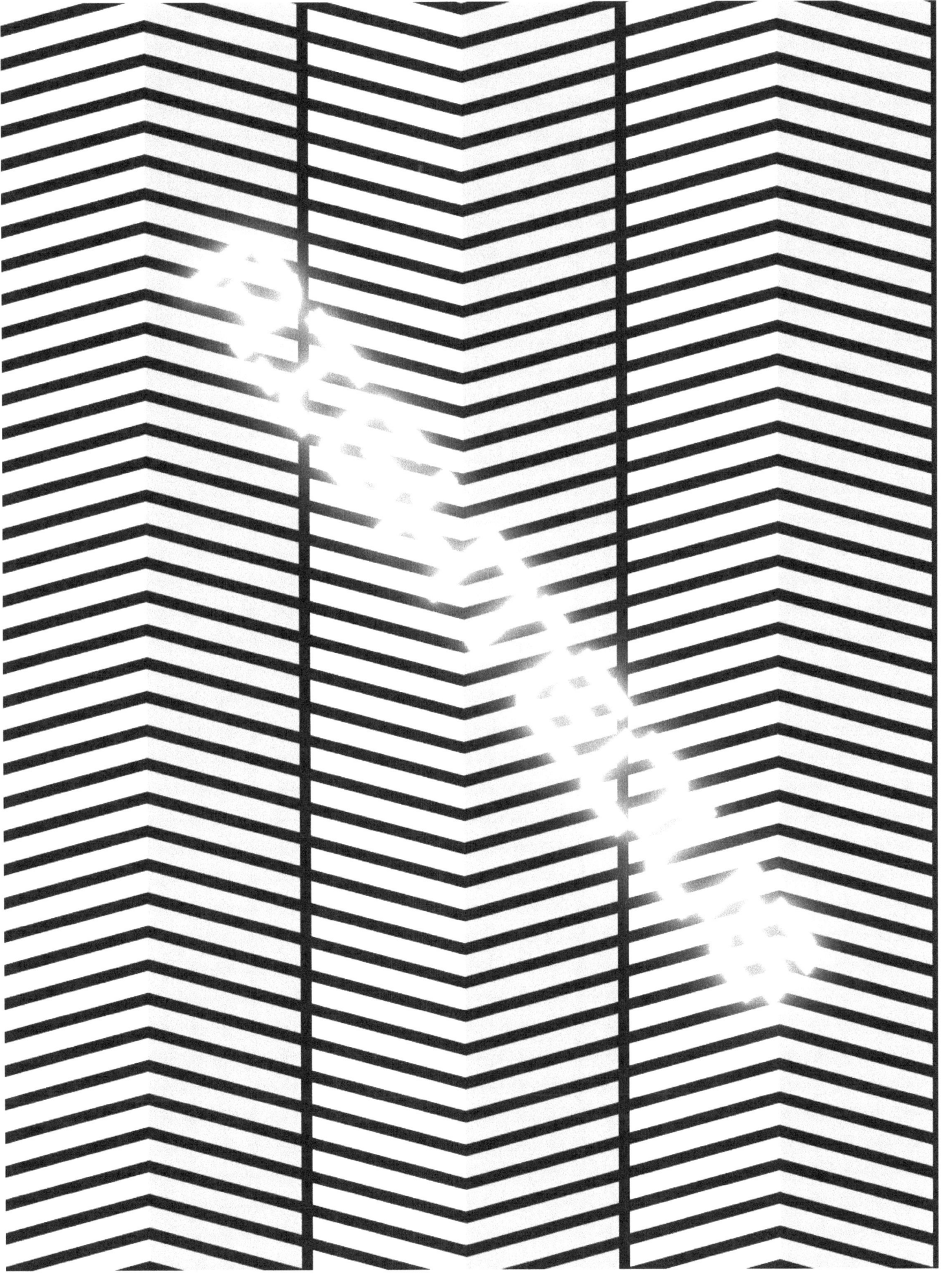

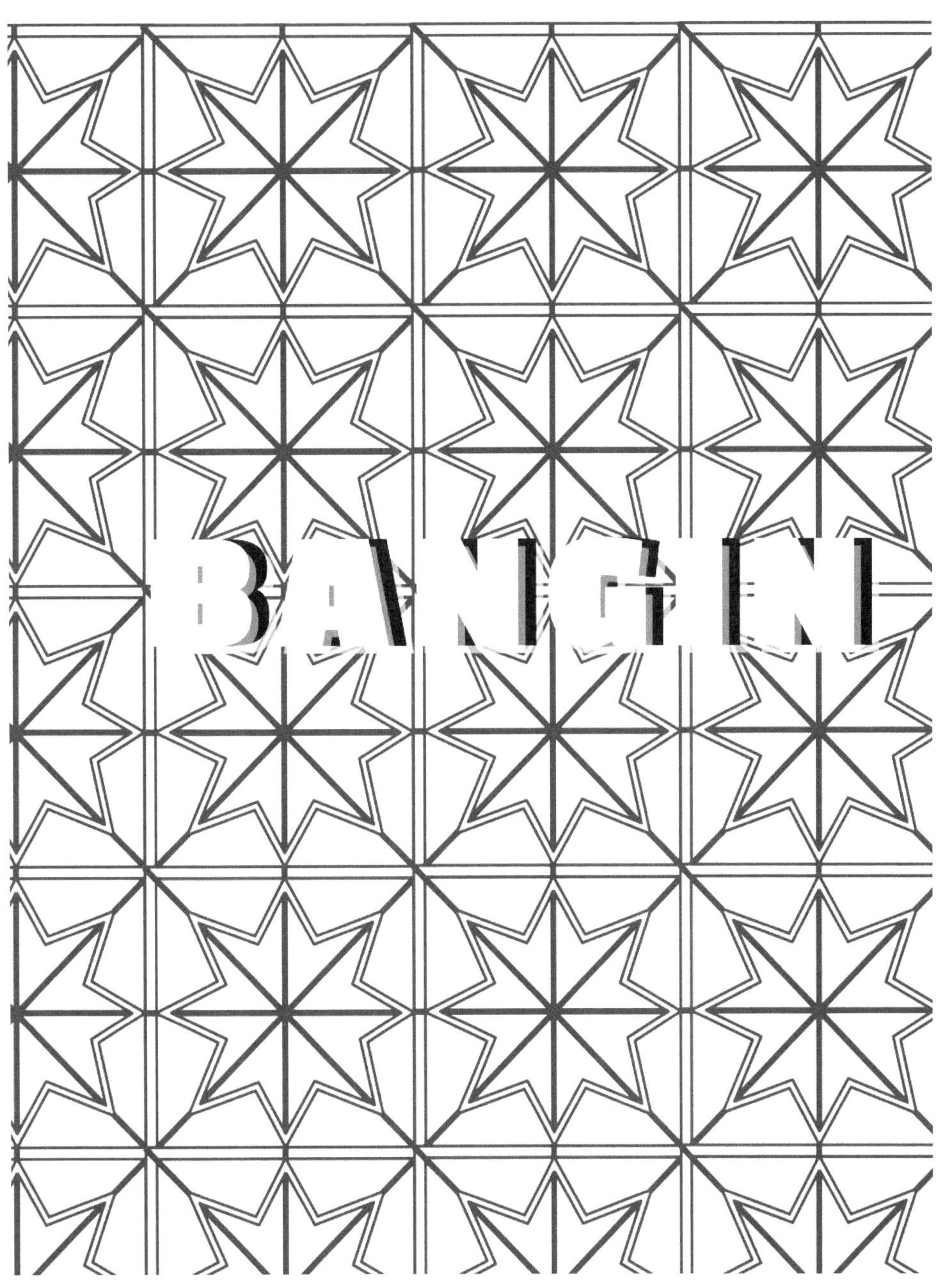

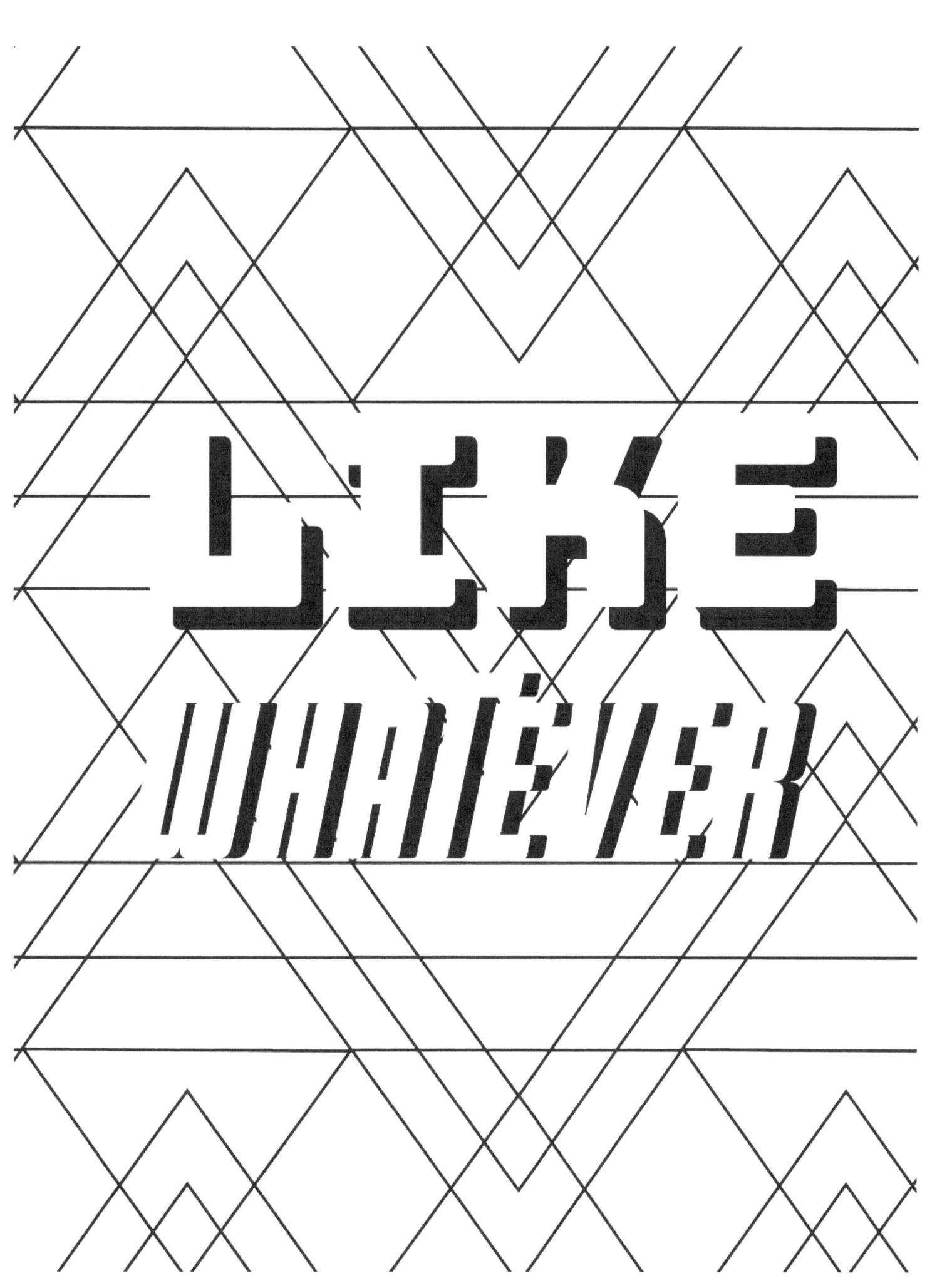

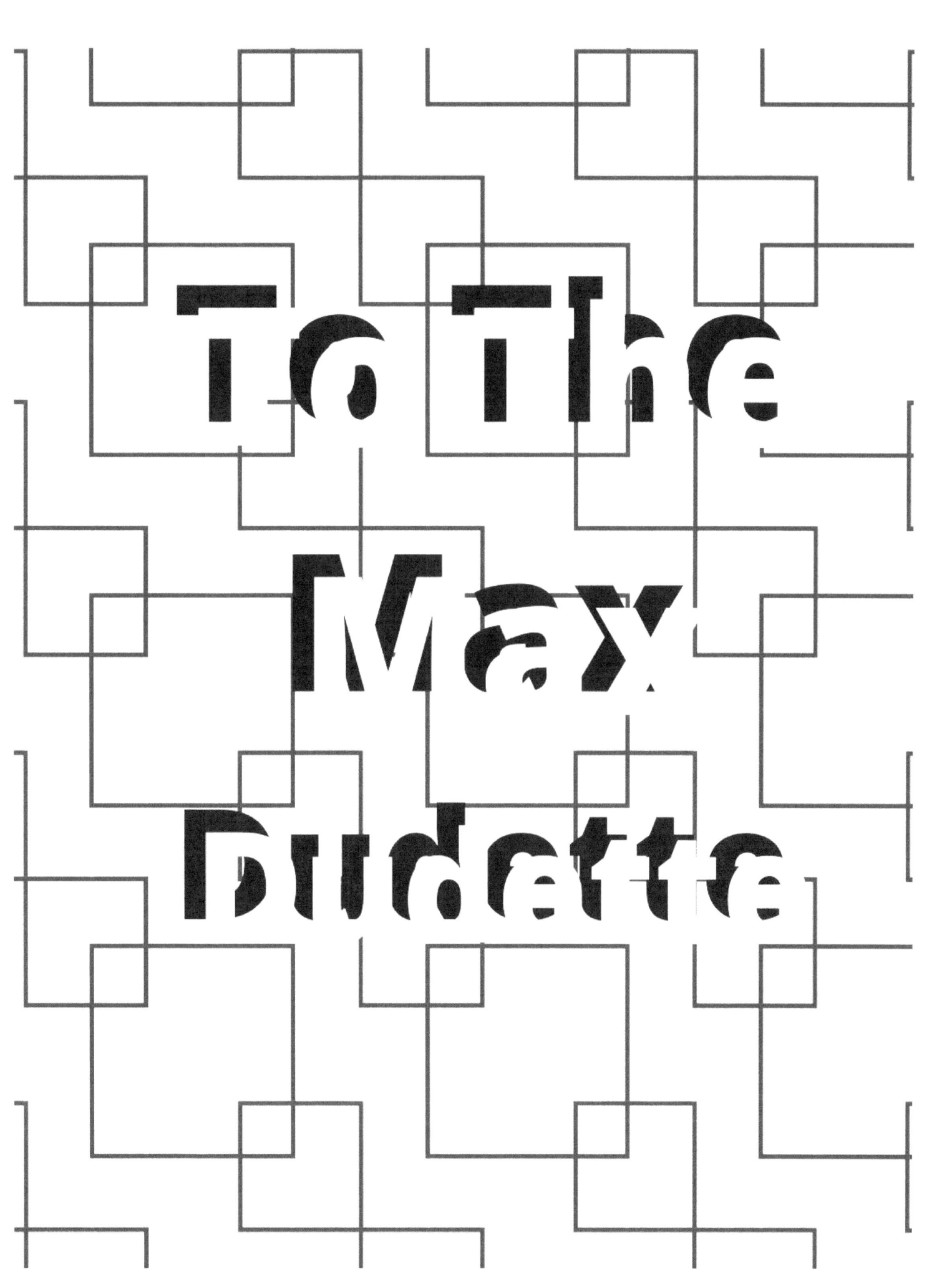

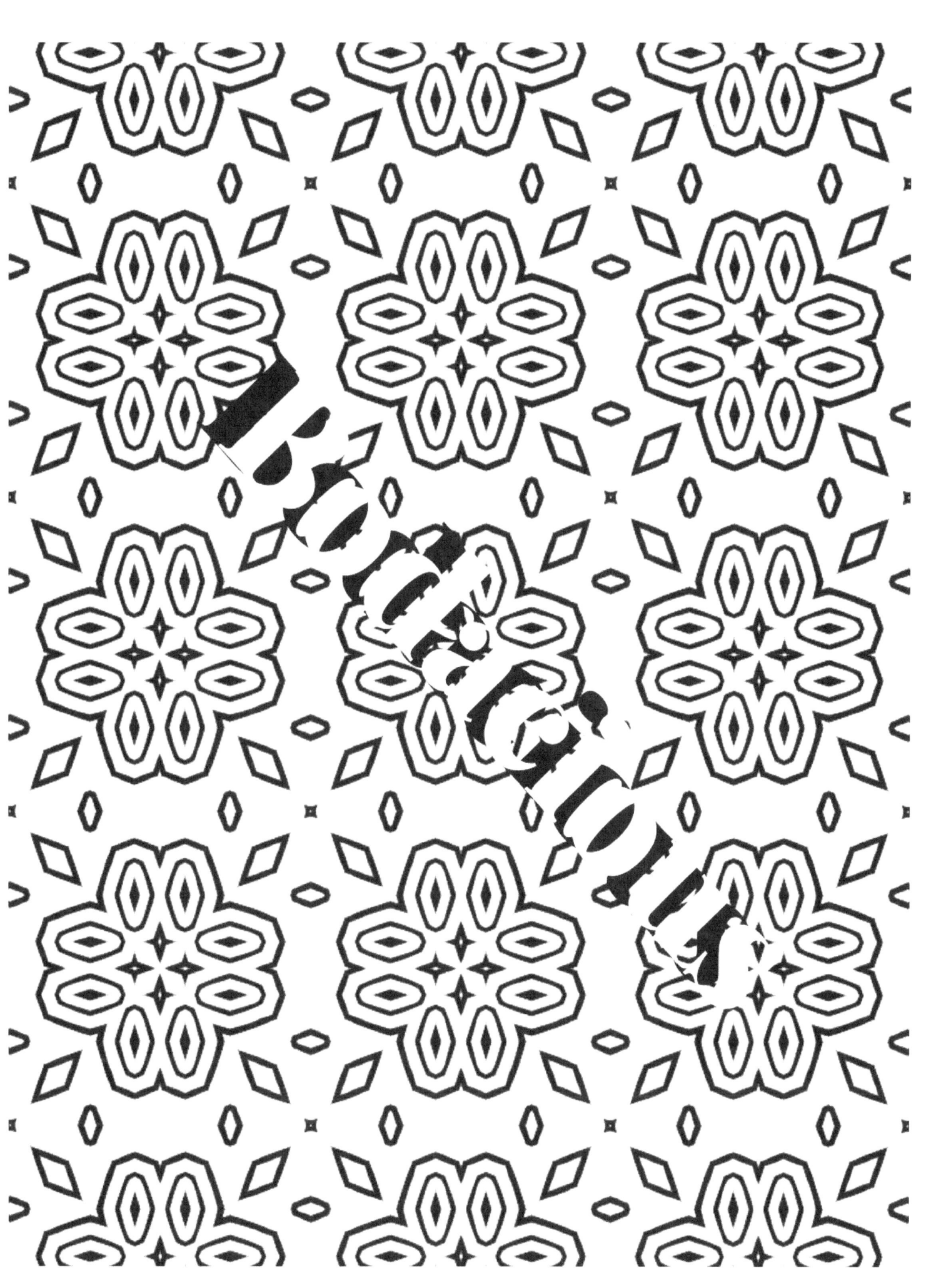

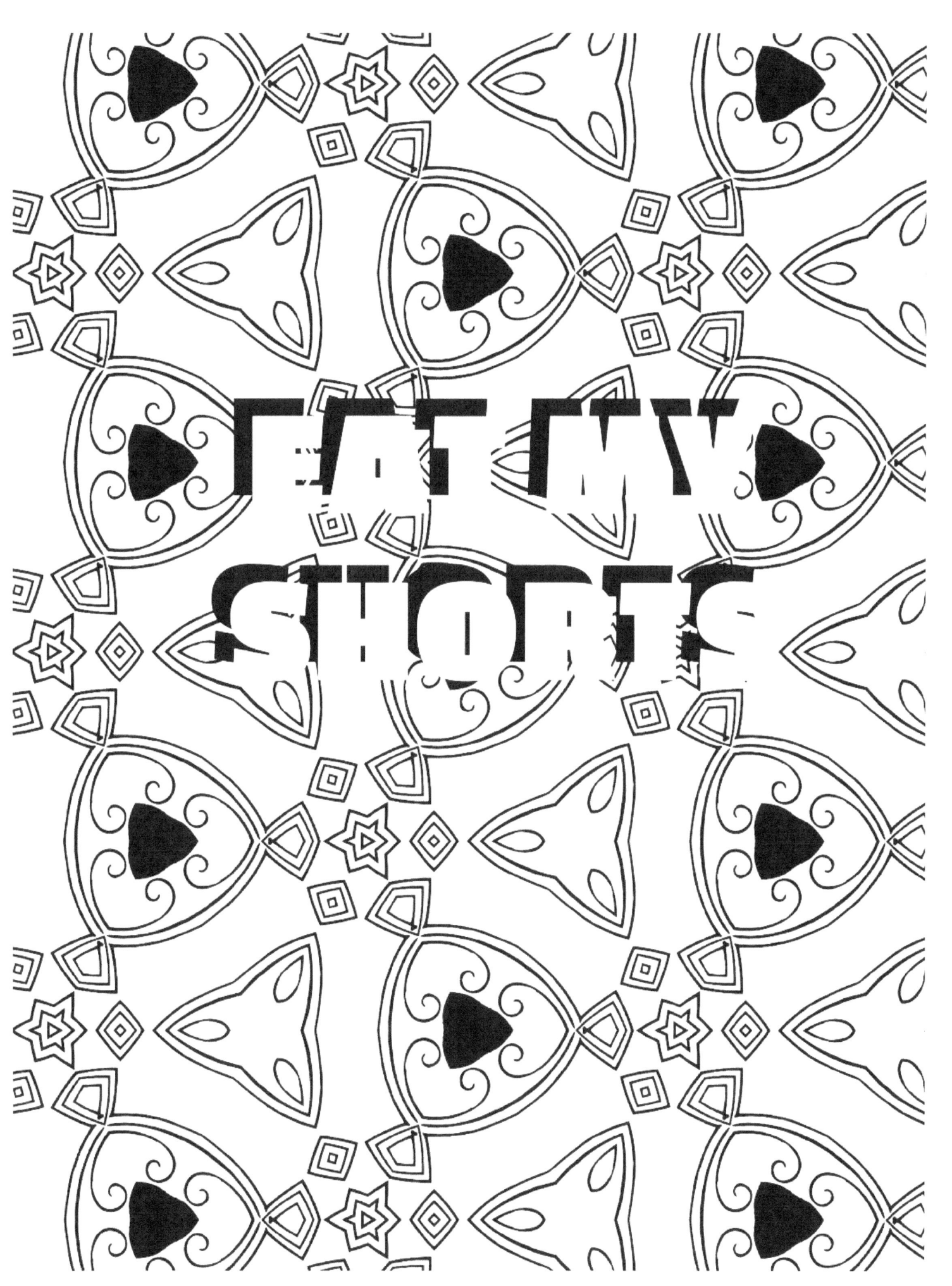

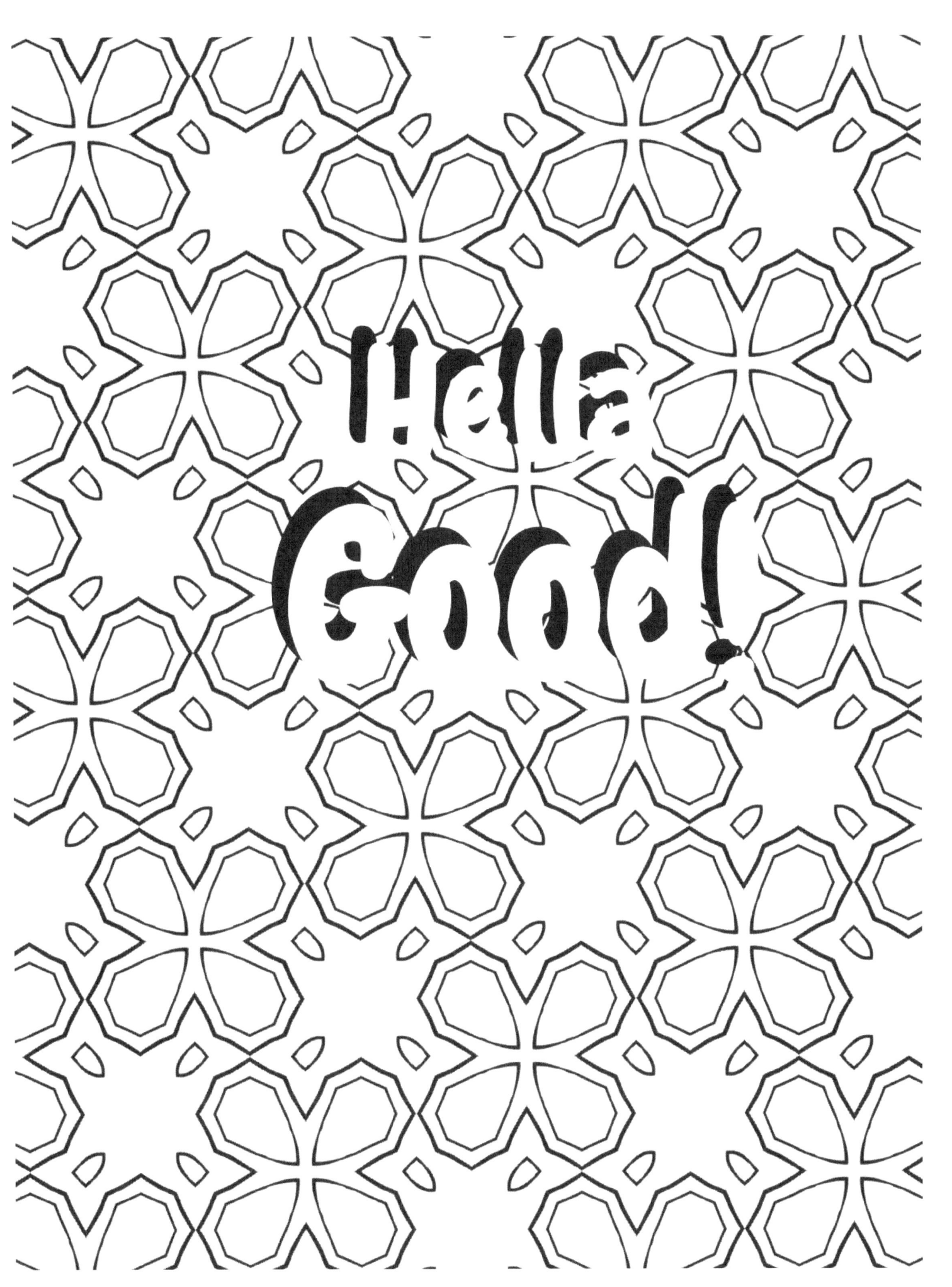

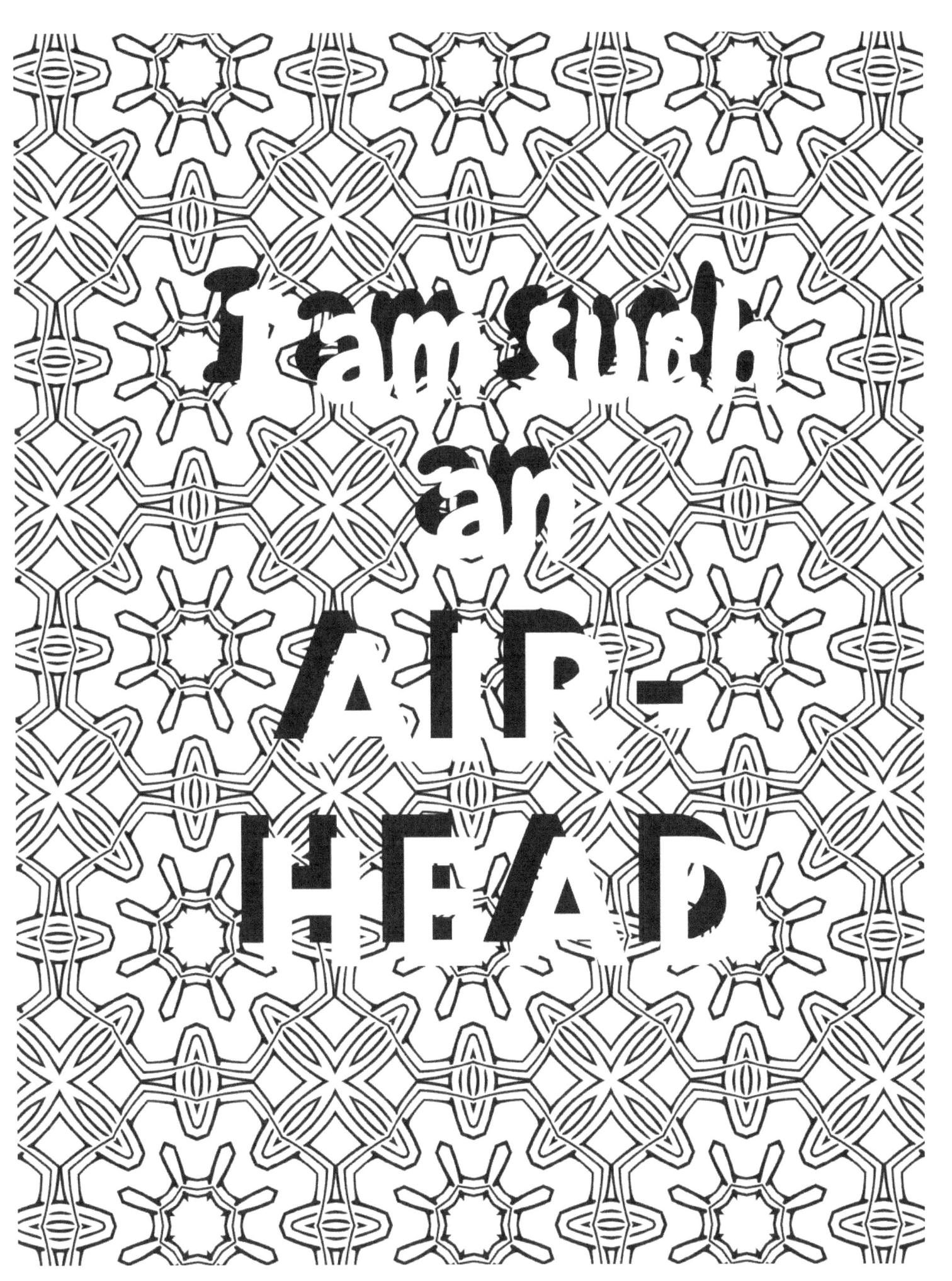

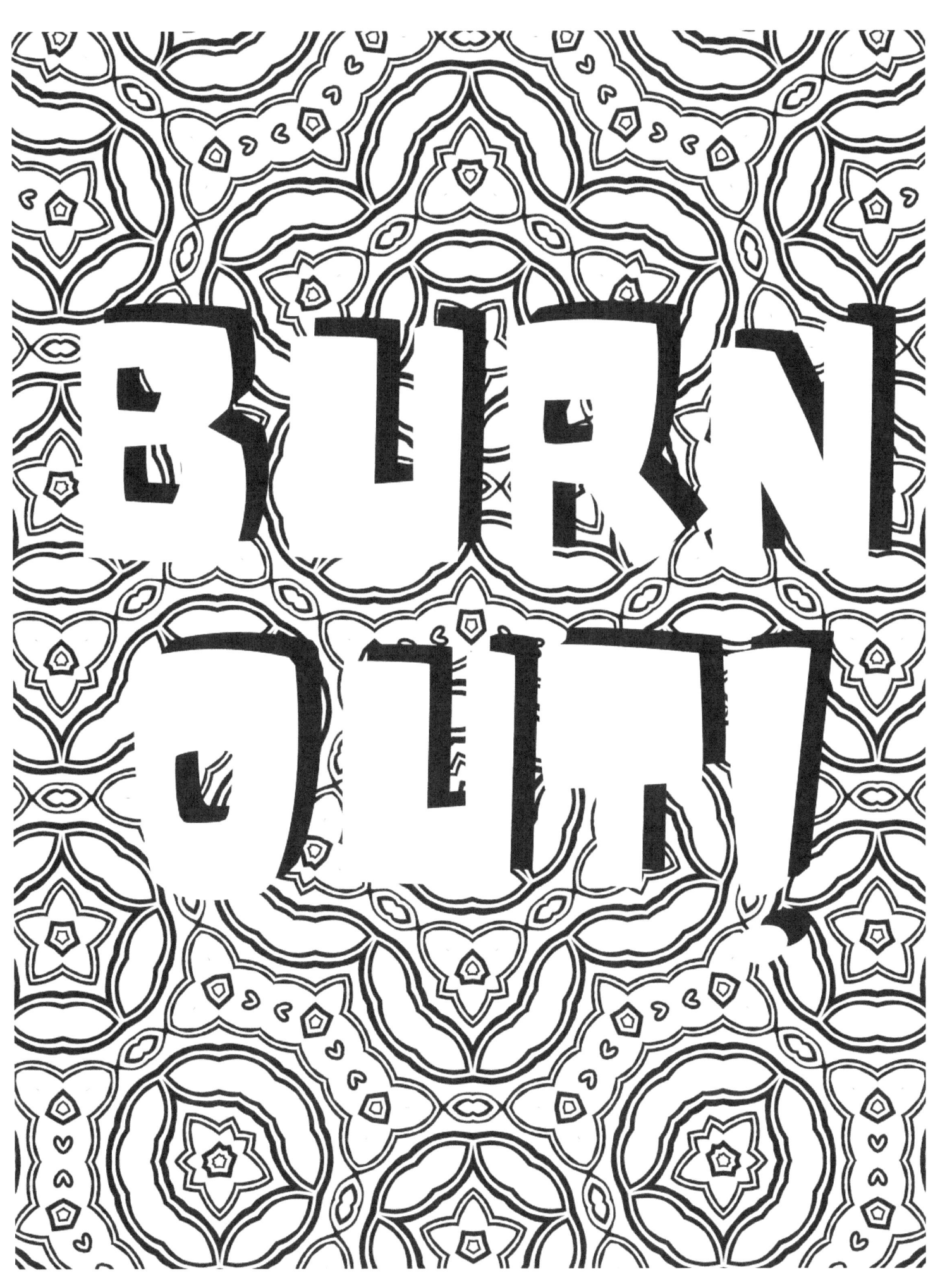

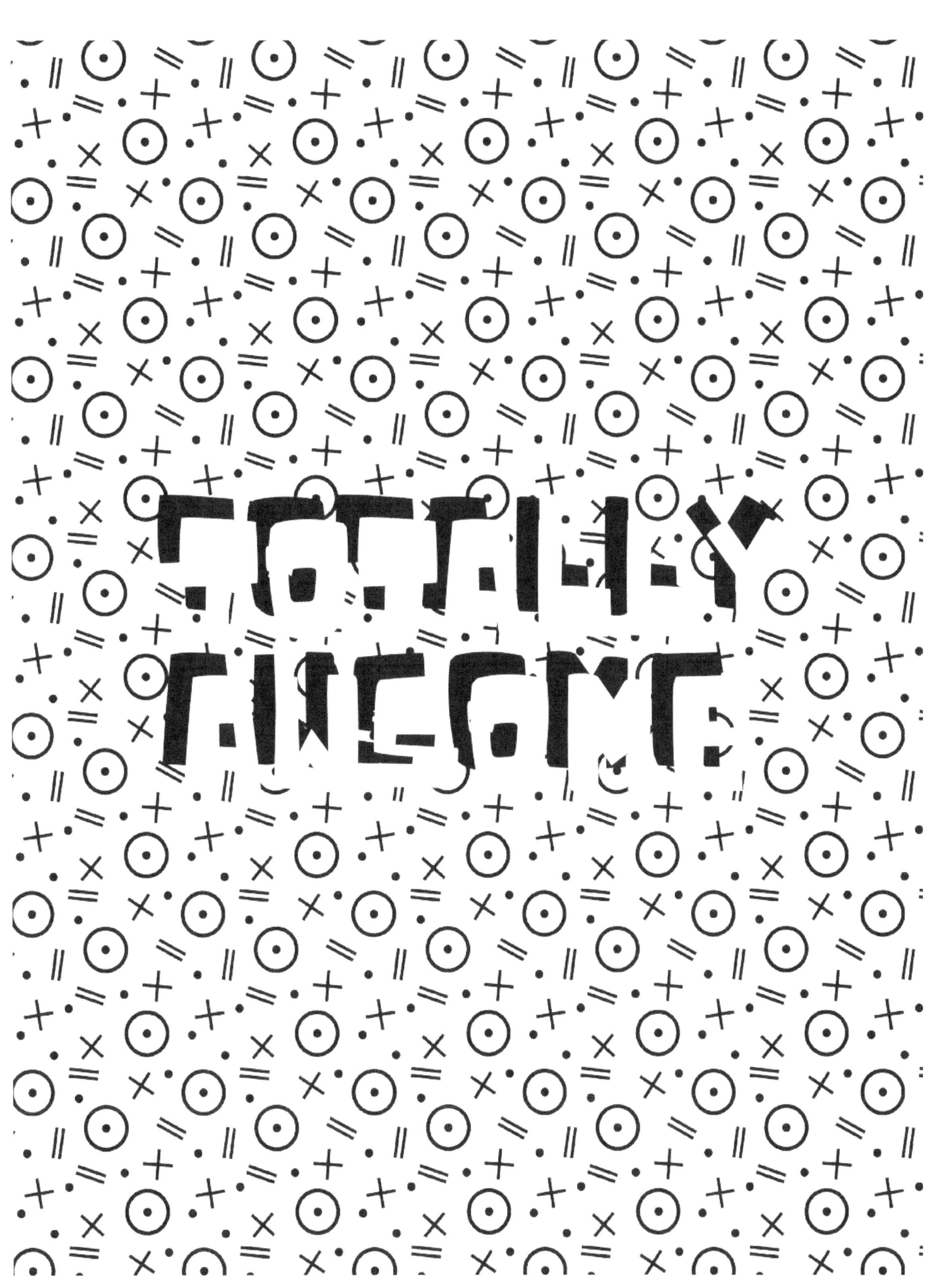

COPYRIGHT 2021

Missy Publishing
Kat Robarge

www.ingramcontent.com/pod-product-compliance
Lightning Source LLC
Chambersburg PA
CBHW060005230526
45472CB00008B/1952